Tulip Fields
of Batavia

AN INCREDIBLE TRUE STORY

Robert Van der Upwich

Tulip Fields of Batavia

Tulip Fields of Batavia

"It's always about what you can do, not where you have been. However, who you are and what you can do is the result of where you have been."

Robert Van der Upwich

**Dedicated to the memory of
Herman and Marie Van der Upwich**

Table of Contents

TULIP FIELDS OF BATAVIA

INTRODUCTION

The Dutch East Indies, or Netherlands East Indies, was formed as a colony of the Netherlands in 1800 when the country nationalized the Dutch East India Company. Expansion included the annexation of the Bird's Head Peninsula in western New Guinea in 1920.

Prior to World War II, the Dutch East Indies produced large quantities of coffee and tea (20% of the world's supply), cacao and coconut (25% of the world's supply), sugar, pepper, tobacco, rubber (35% of the world's supply), quinine (most of the world's supply), and oil (significant portion of the world's supply).

The islands were the Netherland's main source of raw materials. Very little industry existed in the Dutch East Indies. The main interest for the Dutch colonial administration for the colony was trade. The Dutch language was never forced upon the local indigenous population. Instead, the popular Riau dialect of Malay

10

language was the official language so that trade would not be hindered. This official language would later evolve into the modern Indonesian language.

New Guinea is an exotic place, unspoiled and wild. This part of the world is primitive with animal and plant species found nowhere else in the world.

Here's the number of species you will not find outside of New Guinea:

Mammal Species 92
Bird Species 114
Reptile Species 143
Amphibian Species 297
Swallowtail & Butterfly Species 45
Freshwater Fish Species 88
Marine Fish Species 50

The Raggianna Bird of Paradise is the national bird of New Guinea. It's so beautiful; its image is part of the national flag of the country.

Raggianna Bird of Paradise

Dutch East Indies

MY STORY

CHAPTER 1

It is 1954 and only 9 years after the close of World War II in the Pacific. I was born in a rustic clinic 90 miles south of the Equator in the Southern Hemisphere of the planet Earth in a small, undeveloped seaside town called Manokwari. This area in Western New Guinea was an outpost of the Dutch East Indies. In 1947, this area along the northern coast was settled by Dutch and Dutch Indonesian refugees from Java, Indonesia who fled political persecution and violence. They built a life from nothing.

My parents Herman and Marie Van der Upwich, were among this group. He was 36 years old. She was 19. He loved his "sweetheart" very much. She loved her strong protector man. Together they embarked on an adventure and a life that Hollywood could easily bring to the big screen. Their life illustrates the rewards of hard work, perseverance and true grit.

13

Fast forward 66 years. There's some older guy cranking The Doors in a retro 1996 Ford Aerostar van. Oh … that's me! I'm on the way home from another home improvement job with a check in my pocket. My windows are rolled up, but people who pull up at the light next to me look around to see where the music beat is coming from. My wife accuses me of not growing up and I can't help but agree. Guilty!

I'm always reflecting on past years in my life during the height of Rock and Roll, mainly the 60's and 70's. I refuse to move on from that attitude of independence. I loved that period in my life and I still love and live it today. It was freedom and the opportunity to try whatever I wanted. Life was good for a strong young man with hair down to his shoulders. The Vietnam War ended in 1975 and I was never drafted although I had to sign up with the Selective Service System for that possibility in my senior year in high school like a million other guys.

I'm 66 years old now and both of my parents are gone, but I'm still groovin' to Dylan, the Beatles whose music changed the world and the Rolling Stones. I still believe in magic with the Lovin' Spoonful, love Jim Morrison and the Doors, Steve Winwood, Clapton, Elton John, etc.

In my adventurous life, I knew long ago that materialism was not the answer to happiness. It's actually about a lifestyle of freedom and creativity. Oh, and having fun.

Sadly, I have seen too many unhappy people who make big money. According to a Linkedin study in 2018, 7 in 10 people earning over $200K a year were stressed out and had a low feeling of satisfaction and well-being.

My Dad, a simple man, had a philosophy about gainful employment. "Find what you love to do and the money will come naturally". He was right. He was an auto mechanic and he loved cars. He also said,

"Learn a trade with your hands even if it isn't your occupation in case you need it." The education is out there waiting for you to learn on the job you love. All you have to do is develop a marketable skill in a field you enjoy, and you are on your way to a happy working life. Of course it requires the humility to be mentored and be someone's assistant while learning and that's where the positive attitude comes in. I have been working now for 55 years starting with a paper route when I was 11 years old. My mother lied about my age for the paper route. I was a graphic artist and sign painter working out of my garage for 16 years before computers would provide graphics and color reproduction to the masses for inexpensive prices. My past work can be seen in the movie "Thelma and Louise." I finished that career by helping Jay Leno start "Jay Leno's Garage" in the summer of 1992. Two partners and I hand painted the first (8) murals on Jay's car collection /shop walls. That was building #1 that now houses his machine shop from what I see on the show. I believe he has about 6 buildings now.

My second career was 14 years in mortgage banking and real estate sales with an emphasis on refinances and second mortgages. I owned a brokerage with a partner. I thought I would do that the rest of my life until the mortgage crash of 2008. All my friends and associates lost their jobs. The industry was wiped out. I spent 5 years earlier in my life selling hardware, plumbing, electrical supplies and lumber in Northern California. That knowledge allowed me to start being a handyman service which led to a licensed finish carpenter, then a General Contractor now for 12 years. I plan to continue working, but pick only jobs I want. I like making a few bucks and creating things. I am a Shark Tank TV Show fan. I see doctors, lawyers and engineers on that show pitching products they created so they can quit their rat race careers and be entrepreneurs. They all want to be self-employed entrepreneurs. My folks were, and that's where the influence in my life came from. My mother was a very independent, entrepreneurial woman. I can remember Mom pumping gas and wiping windshields at their gas station in

the early 70's in Fountain Valley. She was a
feminist before it became main stream. You
just didn't see women doing that in those
days. She didn't care. She and my Dad
were happy business owners who didn't
have to answer to anyone or care what
they thought. BINGO!

Many people never master the art of
working successfully regardless of
occupation. Remember those bumper
stickers "It's all about attitude"? Those
words are so true. If you show up on time,
you have accomplished 50% of the task. If
you learn how to work efficiently as a team
player, project the right attitude, you get
ahead and you prosper. People will love
you.

Why do I emphasize this topic about
working? Because I grew up with parents
who worked a lot, but seemed happy and
content to do so. They passed that attitude
on to me and I am very grateful to the
point I can't help but share it. Gainful,
satisfying employment has a way of
providing grounding in one's life and a
very important component to successful
living called self-respect. It's what I share

with able bodied street people begging for spare change before they flip me off.

My mom freaked out when I said I was moving to Northern California in 1975 to live in the mountains and experience the rural lifestyle, free of big city demands. She threatened to kill my friend I was going with. Gee, what did she expect? My mother took us camping in the late 1960's to Big Sur, California where we swung on a rope and dropped into a river alongside some folks who were smoking pot, played loud rock music and hadn't had a haircut in a long time. I thought they were pretty cool people and it looked like they were having a great time and doing what they liked. My Mom forgot to check out what kind of people camp at Big Sur before planning our trip. Oh well.

Or what about the time we got lost on a family road trip in San Francisco and wound up in the Haight Ashbury District? There was loud rock & roll, people dancing in the street handing out copies of The Free Press, psychedelic wall murals and rock and roll concert posters everywhere. It was a party!

During my years in Humboldt County from 1975 – 1984, I grew Cannabis for about 3 years. Everybody in Southern Humboldt did. It was illegal, but the state didn't know how to handle it for many years due to ongoing changes in attitudes. One day, four County Sheriff vehicles rolled up on our property in Alderpoint, California. They proceeded to remove about a hundred mature Cannabis plants. I naively offered to be arrested out of protest and admitted to owning the crop. The Sheriff refused to do anything more than "confiscate contraband". I thought if I were arrested, I would have an opportunity to argue against the injustice of it being taken since it was personal property. That was 1977 and it was a felony. Little did I know that the battle would be waged for 40 more years before its use would be treated like beer or wine. I know from personal experience that alcohol is much more dangerous. If any drug should be banned or more severely limited, it should be alcohol. Ask any police officer about alcohol use and domestic violence. I need to add that the local County Sheriff's Lieutenant who was a friend of mine, was arrested a couple of years after he retired for cultivating Marijuana for sale. Irony?

Like I said before, I lived in Humboldt County during some exciting times. This northern part of the state was directly linked to the San Francisco music scene of the late 60's and 70's that defined the hippie movement and the psychedelic generation. The Vietnam War that took the lives of 58,000 Americans, including many who were drafted against their will ended in 1975. America would never force young Americans into military service again under threat of arrest and prison. Remember Mohammad Ali? He was stripped of his heavyweight title, convicted of draft evasion and facing 5 years in prison. He fought that battle for 5 years till the US Supreme Court reversed his conviction. He became an icon for the counter culture, anti-war generation and source of pride for African Americans during the Civil Rights Movement.

That war was the antithesis for the rise of the Love Generation, the Beatles and Dylan. It sparked the liberating, nontraditional attitudes and lifestyles born in the 1960's that continue today. In April 1975, I was driving a U-Haul truck back to California from Michigan. I heard on live radio the reporting of the last U.S. military plane leaving Saigon with people literally hanging on to its exterior to escape the coming North Vietnamese Army. What ensued was the slaughter of millions who were accused of collaborating with or allied with the United States of America. They made a movie about, "Killing Fields". I couldn't help but reflect on the lives of my mother and father who went through similar circumstances and danger in their lives. There is no reason to fight a war overseas against an enemy who is neither attacking your country or even capable of such. In WWII, the free world had to unite to stop the Nazis in Europe and the Japanese Imperial Army in the Pacific. These evil invading forces had already murdered hundreds of thousands of innocent people and would not stop unless destroyed. Both my father and father in law participated in this effort known as the greatest liberation of mankind in history. Both of their stories are stunning and define the bravery and courage of that generation.

These men never met each other, yet they shared that universal human conviction that free people will risk all to remain free. They fought under different flags representing different Allied Forces on opposite sides of the planet, yet their mission was the same. They fought for freedom for good people and against the annihilation of the right to self-determination. Their children and their children's children benefited greatly from these accomplishments. Liberty and the pursuit of happiness were paid forward for generations. God Bless them both.

My father in law Stan Shields saw 154 days of combat. His unit, the 87th Infantry Division was attached to General Patton's 3rd Army, was involved in the Battle of the Bulge and rescued American paratroopers at Bastogne. He was wounded twice, recovered, and still went back to join his unit till the end of the war known as VE Day. He received 3 Bronze Stars for valor and 2 Purple Hearts. This plaque is displayed at Mt. Soledad Veterans Memorial in La Jolla, California in honor of his military service.

STANFORD D. SHIELDS
Staff Sargeant
U. S. Army
World War II

Bronze Star   Combat Infantryman   Purple Heart

MEDALS-RIBBONS: Good Conduct, European-African-Middle Eastern Service w/5 Bronze Stars, World War II Victory

Stanford served with valor in fierce combat for 154 days in the Ardennes, Central Europe and the Rhineland, helping save beleaguered American paratroopers at Bastogne.

Your family forever honors your service

87th Infantry Division

The 87th Infantry counterattack helps to end the siege of Bastogne

EARLY YEARS IN AMERICA

CHAPTER 2

An immigrant is in a nursing home dying. His family is grieving at his side as they watch their beloved patriarch slipping away after years of Alzheimer's disease and failing health. This man worked hard all his life to provide a better future for his family and he succeeded. His children became responsible Americans who also raised their families in the free society he dreamed of and wanted for his loved ones. He lay there quietly as his daughter is holding his hand. Even though his mind and memories had been ravaged by years of Dementia, he softly sang 'God Bless America' before he closed his eyes and slipped away.

My wife is a close friend of this man's daughter. It touched me deeply and reminded me of my own parents who struggled in their lives just to survive. My mother said many times that she and my Dad were just looking to live in a free country where they and their children would not have to leave again under oppression. The ability to work freely, be successful and make a better life for yourself is a precious thing when you've lived under oppression and intimidation. Just ask any Cuban living in South Florida. My Mom and Dad, 3 young children and a newborn baby came to America arriving in Miami in March 1960 after a 3 week journey from Australia through the Panama Canal. Dwight D. Eisenhower was president, but there was a young, charismatic Senator running for president named John F. Kennedy who spoke of a new generation in America and what you can do for your country, not what your country can do for you. My parents were inspired by this Senator from Massachusetts and were firmly on board. We were living in San Antonio, Texas in November 1963. School was let out early the day John F. Kennedy was shot in Dallas. I found my Mom quietly crying by herself in the kitchen when I got home. Our family moved to Huntington Beach in 1964. You could buy a brand new 4 bedroom, 2 bath house with a 2 car garage for $10,900. The down payment was $100.

with a monthly payment of $110. My
father only grossed $90.00 a week working
as a mechanic and pumping gas for Jim's
Union 76 one block from our house. He
worked on cars all his life. His love for the
automobile played an important role in
our family's future as you will see later.
Huntington Beach was home to a big
aerospace & defense contractor McDonnell
Douglas. The home building phenomenon
that began post WWII called tract housing
was alive and well in North Orange
County. In case you don't know, that's
when you build hundreds of new homes at
the same time in stages, offering limited
layouts and sizes repeated throughout the
tract. This type of construction was quicker
and more cost effective than building
individual homes one at a time which prior
to WWII was the norm. If I remember
correctly, our tract had about 4 different
layouts repeated randomly throughout the
evenly spaced streets with cul-de-sac dead
ends. The round, large cul-de-sacs were
our own private ball field, 4th of July
fireworks staging area and 'kick the can'
venue. If you wanted to play basketball,
you had to mount a hoop and a piece of

plywood on the roof of the garage over the driveway, and we did.

During the hot summers of the 1960's, we watched the Beatles come to America, heard daily casualty figures from the Vietnam War on the evening news, saw hippies smoke pot at Woodstock and San Francisco, and watched Neil Armstrong step on the moon all on black and white television. We spent carefree days at the beach where you could park for free anywhere along Pacific Coast Highway, and a big burrito cost 23 cents. There were 3 television networks to choose from for your viewing pleasure in black and white with a roof antenna. When I moved out in 1975, my folks still had a black and white console TV in the living room.

We watched as good men like Martin Luther King Jr., Bobby Kennedy and John Kennedy before them were gunned down by evil men with twisted minds. I watched live the night Bobby Kennedy was gunned down after his speech in Los Angeles. In school, we had to conduct drills that included getting under our desks in case of a nuclear attack from the Soviet Union, and we suffered through countless emergency broadcast patterns on TV during our favorite episodes of Father Knows Best, Bonanza, and Gilligan's Island. Those were interesting times in America, so you can imagine my surprise at later finding out the next door neighbors never liked our family moving into the neighborhood. Unbeknownst to us, they attempted to force us to move by way of a petition that circulated around in our neighborhood. The neighbor across the street who became close friends of our family was personally approached and told my parents. There were still a lot of bigots in America in the 1960's. The Civil Rights Act just passed in 1965. It took two major efforts in Congress to barely pass it. You would think it should be a no brainer. Did I mention we immigrated to the United States in 1960 and looked a little different? My mother was a slender, beautiful dark-haired woman with an olive complexion, and full lips courtesy of a mixed Euro/Indonesian heritage. It was obvious we lacked some sophistication, and my folks were very private people who spoke Dutch as their first language. We kids had a darker complexion due to our island influence and Southern California sun. We looked sort of Hawaiian, but we were not.

I remember trying to talk to my mom about this event, but she didn't want to. She always found it easier to ignore something as if it never happened than address it. It was a trait I promised myself I would not adopt in my own life. The unintended consequence was feeling dismissed, but I always felt loved and encouraged by her. She was the product of a vicious war, poverty, fear and yes, discrimination. Later in life, I fully understood why she avoided conflict.

My Dad was European, mostly Dutch born and raised in Indonesia and barely spoke English. He was 17 years older than my mother and he adored her. He always called her his sweetheart. I had the room across the hall from them and I remember hearing my mother giggling at night from behind their bedroom door. I didn't know what that was till later in life.

My mother and father met and wed in 1946 less than a year after he was liberated as a POW in Burma. At the same time, she gained her freedom as a civilian after 3.5

years of Japanese military occupation and food shortages in the islands. Even civilians were prisoners in their own land. It wasn't the first time my parents dealt with race and class warfare. At least this time, their lives weren't at risk because of it. I will get into that later. It was however my first experience with bias, and even as a youngster I understood it to be insulting and frankly made me look at my neighbors with disbelief at their stupidity. After all, their son and I were friends. What's with these people anyway? This was the 1960's man! Get with it!

I had another neighbor across from us on a perpendicular street who used to taunt me by telling me our family looked like a bunch of Ubangi's. His last name was Holsinger, so whenever I saw him, he was addressed with a new first name, "Ass" to go with his last name Holsinger. I had a knack for firing right back and not having a lot of patience for low IQ individuals.

I learned early that a bully is actually a coward. We had a bully named Billy in the neighborhood who intimidated and harassed kids for some time because he could. There was a point in my life, probably the 7th grade where I realized I was pretty capable of defending myself. So one day Billy stopped my friend and I on the sidewalk a block from my house. He wanted to get tough and threatened us, so I let him have it. He was shocked and cried like a baby after I pummeled him. That was the end of Billy's reign of terror. He was a nice kid after that.

MANOKWARI YEARS

CHAPTER 3

This story is dedicated not only to my parents, but to the whole Dutch-Indo community who courageously endured a brutal war, survived oppressive occupation in their homeland and lost everything. They never gave up dreaming of a life where they and their children could live in freedom and liberty. I am my parents dream and so are others in similar circumstances. We are the succession of their lives, their faith, their hope and hard work.

There is an old handmade wood plaque in my office today that hung in the dining room of my parent's home as long as I can remember. This wood plaque was brought over from New Guinea when our family immigrated to the United States. It says "Hijt niet bezorgd" in Dutch. Translated it means "Don't Be Concerned". The message is "have faith, things will get better." My Mom told me this was the anthem of hope adopted by the civilian population in the Dutch East Indies after the invasion and occupation of Java by the Japanese Imperial Army who brutalized the civilian population.

Ironically, I am writing this during the pandemic known as Coronavirus that has swept the planet and will end up taking as many lives as a war, so the same message is still relevant today.

Life in the Dutch East Indies was close to paradise, a place still talked about and relived in the hearts and minds of those who were there. The years have taken some of those hearts and minds including my parents, but their story lives on in these pages and the numerous texts of recorded history.

The Netherlands East Indies, or Dutch East Indies as it was known, is identified as the island nation of Indonesia today. Located near the equator, the East Indies possessed the warmest trade winds. I can still remember those tall, swaying coconut palms that are the symbol of many tropical locales throughout the world. Exotic fruit grew wild in the jungles bordered by untamed rivers and coastlines. The indigenous Indonesian people lived in harmony with Europeans as employees and extended families, primarily the Dutch. Europeans mingled with the island inhabitants for generations, married the beautiful native women and had children. Hence, the Indonesian influence with European surnames. This was their permanent home for generations before the Japanese Imperial Army invaded in 1942 and right after the attack on Pearl Harbor, Hawaii on December 7, 1941. We've all heard about the cruelty exerted on civilians and prisoners by the Japanese Army. As I once read, imagine how bad it could have been and know that what you can imagine was true.

My childhood memories include watching outrigger canoes ride the waves and playing in the warm South Pacific waters. One day, a land mine went off down the beach that was buried under the sand and seriously injured a man who mistakenly built a wood fire on top of it. The buried land mine had been left unexploded from the war. I was about 4 years old, and remember it as a frightening experience. Our simple, stucco house on a dirt road was connected to a store in front. My parents owned and operated a mercantile that sold durable goods and food staples in Manokwari, New Guinea. In later years, you could find a couple of scooters for sale as well. The store and home were built by my dad, friends and local natives. The home had open windows with no glass because there was no glass available. They hung roll down blinds or curtains for privacy.

Evenings at home included gatherings of friends from the area who shared Gilbeys Gin and also played music. My folks were popular. My father, a Dutch Infantryman with the KNIL was a talented mechanic and respected by his peers for surviving the labor camps as a POW in Burma during the war. My mother was a savvy merchant who was a beautiful young woman of European and Indonesian heritage. She was 17 years his junior. My parents also owned and operated a small chicken farm right down the road in Wosie. I remember going with my father in our VW bus to feed and sometimes take a chicken or two back for dinner.

My father and his friends pulled an old Japanese troop carrier out of the jungle and cleaned it up. The local school needed a bus since the school was located up a dirt road above town. My Dad told me they needed a distributor cap to make it run. It was a 4-cylinder motor and of course there wasn't access to one. He found a distributor cap that fit but was an 8-cylinder type, so he had to plug 4 of the holes to make it work.

I have a memory of my dad taking me to soccer games played on a local dirt field. Decades later he would often mention his regret of not pursuing the sport more in his own life. He loved soccer. Soccer is the most popular sport in the world. My apologies to NFL fans.

That is me. Manokwari school picture 1958

Manokwari, where I was born, is located on the northern coast of New Guinea and was just a rustic small town built and established by Dutch-Indo refugees from Java, Indonesia. My parents were born on Java. The island nation of Indonesia had been a Dutch colony for 150 years and known then as the Dutch East Indies. The islands were rich in agriculture, mainly coffee and tea. My parents and many others of European descent fled Java under threat of forced property seizure and violence after the war ended. This was 1946, a year after the atomic bomb was dropped on Hiroshima and Nagasaki to end the Japanese military reign of terror in the South Pacific that included the Philippine Islands and Southeast Asia. When my parents fled Java, they took three bags of clothes, bedding, two baby pigs, two chickens and a rooster. They boarded a boat and made the journey to a new life across the sea. Indonesia had been re-assigned to the indigenous people and their new leader, a dictator named Sukarno. This was a settlement negotiated in post war proceedings in the newly formed United Nations. Upon this new order, some local indigenous vigilante groups took it upon themselves to forcibly take property and assets from anyone. This was a period of chaos known as the "changeover" and was marked by nightly raids of murder sprees and burning of homes and businesses. They didn't have guns. They used machetes to kill.

The Dutch government, still weak from the war, could only offer limited help by opening Western New Guinea as a destination choice to those needing to leave. My Dad kept a souvenir from the war. His Mauser pistol was always close by.

The other option was to immigrate to the Netherlands and take your chances in a war-torn country. The Netherlands had been bombed and occupied by the Nazi's and the country was under reconstruction and chaotic.

The people who chose to venture to New Guinea were brave and determined to salvage the only life they had known before 1942. Coming from the tropics, many hated the cold European climate and yes there was bias towards people of Javanese roots. My mother avoided the Netherlands for those reasons. Of course that does not exist today, but it was a different world in the 1940's. Many of these people settled later in the Orange County/LA area and would gather weekly at a club in Anaheim to reminisce about their past lives in the Dutch East Indies and enjoy camaraderie with old friends from that life. I knew and met a few of them. I had gone to the club a few times with Mom in the 1990's. These are the friendliest, kindest people you would ever meet, but I saw a quiet sadness and longing for the life they once knew and loved, even after 40 years. These are people without a place to call their homeland. Their homeland was taken away from them.

Many went to Holland where Dutch is the country's national language. However, Dutch from Indonesia were treated more like foreigners than compatriots and often referred to as "Brown Dutchmen." This drove many to migrate elsewhere across the world, including the USA and Australia. I have an uncle in Australia. The US Census Bureau recorded a total of about 60,000 Dutch citizens arriving in the United States between 1950 and 1965. This community of people had been reluctant to share their traumatic history with their children, so they encouraged the next generation to fully embrace American life and ideals. I know my parents did not speak much about their history in Indonesia with their children. Many things I learned while doing the research for this project were new to me. I'm just glad my mother talked more as she got older and I became more interested. I always thanked her for the opportunity to travel with her in 1995 to Indonesia. It truly was a trip of a lifetime to a beautiful place and fed more into my curiosity about our family history and the history of an entire society that no longer existed in its homeland and why.

MARIE ANTOINETTE

CHAPTER 4

My mother always liked to point out her famous name. Her birth name is Marie Antoinette Chompff. It was appropriate for a beautiful girl. My mother was one **of** 10 children. Her mother Ida, had her first child at 16. This was not uncommon in those times and neither were arranged marriages or marriage between older men and younger women. My mother's childhood was very tough and included factors that would normally result in tragedy.

The following is her story in her own words written at the age of 77 in 2005.

As she wrote:

"I was born in Situbondo, a small town in East Java. My dad [Christiaan Albert Chompff] was working on a sugar plantation [as a bookkeeper], and the worker's families could not stay at the plantation; there was not housing, therefore they rented a house in the nearest town. In my case that was Situbondo.

My mother, Ida Mathilde Wilhelmina
Werdmuller von Elgg (Ida Chompff) was
16 years old when her first baby was born:
Johanna Theodora. I was the second baby.
My nickname was Zus (it means little sister
because I had an older sister). When I got
a little older (about 14 or 15) my nickname
was Tjanga ("stick") because I was so
skinny.

But when I was born, my mother called a
fortune-teller (a lot of people did that) to
tell the future of the baby. It was nonsense
of course, but custom in that part of the
world. The fortune teller told my mother:
"This baby should have been a boy." My
mother asked why. She said this baby will
always be a merchant, or be in that kind of
business (a business person!). Buy and sell
goods or whatever.

Then came the big Depression of 1930
(which was worldwide), my father became
unemployed. We all moved to Pekalongan
in Central Java, where he got a job as a
bookkeeper. There was a river near the
house. We used to play there--my 2 sisters,
Christine and Johanna, and me. One day I
almost drowned. My sisters Christine and
Johanna told me this story of drowning a

lot of years later (in my 50s). I can't even remember it myself.

I was 7 years old, when my dad died of a heart attack on January 7, 1936. After my dad died, all I can remember was poverty, a lot of it. I had no toys to play with. In all my life I had one old, secondhand doll. On my 12th birthday I got a rusty second hand bicycle to go to school (high school). I never had a birthday celebration, till after the war, when I turned 18. And even that turned disastrous! Nothing but poverty all my childhood, in a slum area.

I remember telling my husband, "I will never be that poor again in my life." That is why I always save money. I felt all my life, that it was the only way to stay out of poverty! Money in the bank! Save, save, save, and be careful when you spend it! I have to have money in the bank, or I would feel very insecure!!

My mother was pregnant when my father died and named the baby boy after him, Christiaan Albert. But the baby also died. He died of dysentery at about 1 or 2 years old.

Soon after my father's death, Johanna and me, were put in Catholic boarding at the convent in Batavia, because my mother had no income and she was too proud to accept welfare. She told me this later on, years later, when we were in the United States already. The convent was all Catholic, the street was "Noordwyk", all female nuns. We called them sister or mother depending on their rank. One of the nuns was an aunt or cousin of my father, tante (aunt) Dora. We stayed there for 1 year (till January 1937). This boarding school was free for us. It was okay and we were treated nice. They even gave us new clothes. I was there in the 3rd grade, and part of 4th grade. The nuns had new names for us. Johanna was renamed "Dora". I was renamed "Netty".

I was always sick with bronchitis and therefore the nuns decided for us to move to another climate, because Batavia has a real hot and muggy climate. We were moved to another Catholic convent in Bandung, a city in the mountains of West Java, on Houtmanstraat (street name), where the climate was more pleasant! We stayed there more than 3 years (my 4th, 5th, 6th, and part of 7th grade—elementary schools had 7 grades).

Soon after we (Johanna and me) arrived I noticed that this was a real orphanage, with 230 girls of all ages. The nuns were not as nice as in the other convent and there were also girls, whose parents paid for them to be there (like a boarding house) because the parents were living on the plantations around the town. I believe the plantations were sugar, rubber, and tea. There were no schools at the plantations, only homes for the employees.

I notice that in this orphanage we all had numbers (because there were 230 girls, I guess). My number was 47 and my sister Dora [Johanna] was number 66. Also, we had no rooms to sleep in. Sleeping was on folding beds, all in a long row in a large area, one folding bed after another, and next to another. In other words, there was no privacy for anybody. When it was time to sleep, everybody got on their own bed, and we had to be quiet, because the nuns were walking up and down the aisles, to make sure we were all behaving. There were showers built next to the sleeping area, a whole row of showers with curtains, one next to another.

If we had stuff from home that we wanted to put away, there was only 1 small chest of drawers per person. This was in the area where we had to brush our teeth and wash our faces.

The chest had a bowl on top with a faucet, and below there were 3 drawers where you can put your personal stuff in. No locks! Everything was unlocked. And your number (#47) was on the chest so you know which one of the drawers is yours. The school was right there, and then there was a long hall (covered) that led to the church. The nuns had the convent by the church, so we had only a few [nuns] at a time, to watch over us in shifts, then they went back to their convent that was built next to the church. You had to walk the long, long hall to get there.

For summer vacation, Dora [Johanna] and I were put on the train, and we had to go to my mother in Batavia, and there we had to help her with her sewing for her customers. She was a seamstress, and the ladies (her customers) came to the house to see her and then she made the clothes at home on her sewing machine. Dresses mainly. At the end of the summer vacation

(6 weeks was the summer vacation) we were put on the train (train ride was 3 hours) back to Bandung and the orphanage.

I was in the 7th grade, and had just turned 12-years-old (January 1940) when one of the "paying" girls, whose parents had paid for her to be there in the orphanage, had a birthday and the parents came over and gave her a gold pen for her birthday present. Anyway, a few days later, the pen was gone, and this girl went to the nuns and told them that I had stolen the pen. I was called and escorted to a room with three nuns around me, interrogating— where is the pen? What did I do with it? I did not have the pen—I was wrongly accused! But, of course, the nuns believed the girl, because she was a paying guest! Then they told me, if I was lying I had to go to jail for stealing. I still denied I had the pen. Then they said the jail was full of spiders and mice, not a nice place. I still denied it. Then one of the nuns went into another room and pretended she was calling the police. She spoke so loud that I could hear her say: "Is this the police?" And then she said there was a girl here that had stolen a pen. After she hung up, she came back and told me, the police were on the way to pick me up.

I was so scared, I said, "OK, I stole the pen." I thought, anything but the jail with the mice and spiders. That was a stupid thing I did, but of course, I was only 12-years-old, and not thinking of the consequences that followed. Now I had to produce the pen that I did not have! Now they thought that I was being stubborn and dishonest, and they felt I had to be punished!

I got locked up in a small room, the size of a bathroom. There was a table and a chair in the room, a toilet and a sink. I had to do math all day long—multiplication from number 1 to forever. For fresh air, there were a few window blinds way up near the ceiling, 3 or 4 glass blinds, that you can open for air, and close if you want to. It was so high, I had to climb on the chair, to reach it. I was locked up 2 or 3 weeks (can't remember exactly). A nun came 3 times a day with food. Rice, salt, a glass of water. That was all I got. At night, bedtime, I was not allowed to sleep on the floor where everyone slept. I had to sleep in the shower

51

stall, with a mattress on the floor. They
wanted me completely separated from the
rest of the girls, in isolation.
One time I climbed on the chair, and
looked through the blinds, and I saw a girl
from my class. I had written a letter to my
mother, but I had no stamps. I asked her if
she could mail the letter for me to my
mother. This girl was not staying at the
orphanage. She was there only at school,
and went home after school. She took my
letter and went straight to the nuns. That
was not very nice. I was confronted with
that fact, by the nuns!
After 2 or 3 weeks, suddenly, they picked
me up and put me in another room, where
they fed me meat, potatoes, veggies. It
tasted real good after all that rice and salt. I
was very surprised, but they still said
nothing! After a few days of good food,
suddenly they took me to the train station
with a one-way ticket to Batavia, where my
mother lived. She picked me up and I told
her the story of my isolation. The school
year ended a few months later (in June),
and I stayed home with my mother (no
school). My sister Dora (Johanna), came
home in June from the orphanage and I

asked her if the pen was ever found? She said, "Yes." Another girl had stolen the pen. But I never heard anything from the orphanage anymore, after those years!

I went to high school in the town where my mother lived (Batavia) everyday, back and forth on my rusty old bike.

In May 1940, Germany (Hitler) invaded the Netherlands and all contact with the islands of Indonesia [Dutch colonies] were broken. Four months after Pearl Harbor was attacked by Japan in April 1942, the Japanese invaded the Indonesian islands. During those four months, every time when we heard the sirens, we had to crawl under the bed. Sometimes I heard bombs fall around us. I was living with my mother.

After the invasion, all the schools closed. I was in high school a year and a few months of the second year, when the school closed. My mother was in a welfare house, where every family gets 1 room for the whole family. I was 14 years old and the Japanese told me I was too old to be at home with my mother. I had to leave and fend for myself. They said, at 14 you are an adult—go find a job.

I found a job (in the evening from 6-10 pm), keeping score for Japanese men, in a billiard hall. The school in the neighborhood was closed but the Japanese opened one classroom and put a pool table in there. I had to keep score while 4-5 men played pool. They never tried anything inappropriate with me, I must say. During the Japanese occupation of the islands, our military men were shipped to Siam (now called Thailand) to work on the "bridge over the river Kwai," because the Japanese Emperor needed a short route to the ocean that was bordering Thailand. He needed that for shipping purposes from Japan to the ocean (I think it was the Indian Ocean—not sure). I remember how we all rushed to the train station, whenever a rumor went around that a transport of the men was coming to the station. The trains never stopped at the station, they only went through to a destination somewhere near the ships that had to bring them to Thailand. But while they were going through the station, we were standing on the side, to wave at the prisoners of war. We could see the faces of the men behind the glass windows. They were not allowed to open the windows to wave back. All we saw were the sad faces behind the glass windows—a sight that has never left my memory of war experiences. Thousands of our men went to Thailand (as prisoners of war). During the Japanese occupation of the islands, real food was hard to get for the people that were not in the camps. In certain parts of the islands, the Japanese had put the families in camps. They were not allowed to leave. The food was rationed by the Japanese. This is what I heard—I was never in a camp. The food was really bad, but survivable, is what they told me. Anyway, I was among the people not in the camp, trying to survive on my own.

That was the time when I met Frits. I was 15 or 16 years old, can't remember. Frits knew that the Japanese had picked up girls of my age from the street, and transported to the other islands for prostitution for their army men, but I did not know that. He was always hovering over me, making sure that he was with me, whenever I had to go somewhere. Later in my life, is when he told me why he always did that. I believe I owe Frits my life. Without him, I might not be alive. His family, his sisters and brothers who were all older than me, had taken care of me, as often as needed. I owe his whole family my life (the De Jong family).

The food was real bad, because all the good food went to the Japanese occupiers. We had to eat "dideh", which was the blood from the animals when they were slaughtered. The beef goes to the Japanese. The civilians had to eat "dideh" (blood mixed with vinegar turns a little hard and looks like "red tofu"). There was no beef, chicken, bread, or milk whatsoever available—only the dideh and the roots, like sweet potatoes and rice. No milk at all! No bread!

The end of the war came finally but we had to fight another war. The Indonesian people wanted their country back from Dutch colonization, and an "uprising" started against the Dutch government. They wanted us out! We were all Dutch citizens because when we were born, the islands were Dutch territory, and our last names were descendants of Dutch fathers. So, we won one war, but went straight into

56

another war, with a different enemy: the Indonesians in August 1945 right after the atomic bombs were dropped on Nagasaki and Hiroshima.

During the uprising, the Indonesians did their bidding at night. They had no guns, only machetes, long knives that can kill just the same. Therefore, at night we all had to sleep on the rafters inside the house. We had to climb up to the rafters, by the way of a long ladder, only 3 of the men of Frits' family stayed in the living room with guns, protecting the family on the rafters. These 3 men were Frits, and his brothers Ben and Carl. The Indonesians were always avoiding the house, because they knew that those 3 men had guns, and they had only the machetes. Later on (years later), I learned from Ben how they got the guns.

Here is Ben's story: After the Japanese lost the war, they (Japanese soldiers in the town) ran away from their post and had left their guns and ammunition behind. They were afraid we would hang them because of all the cruelties they had committed to us all. Ben and his brothers (Frits and Carl) heard about it and rushed to the Japanese posts and found the weapons sitting there. They picked them up to protect the family from the Indonesians. A lot of Dutch people were killed by Indonesians after the war with Japan, slaughtered with their machetes. There was lawlessness everywhere, no security, only confusion. No protection from the uprising, because our military men were still in Thailand and Japan where they were held as prisoners of war and had not gone home yet, for whatever reason. The United Nations military arrived before our own army men. Finally, after a few months, our own military came home from overseas (where they were prisoners of war), and slowly our lives went back to a normal life. I remember when the Americans came in (to help us), standing in a long line for rations. Each one got a loaf of bread, 2 cans of sardines, chili con carne, corned beef, etc. It was food anyway. We did not have to eat the blood from animals anymore. What a relief that was. Slowly the schools were opened again, and we could walk on the streets without fear of being stopped by Japanese army men. The cruelty stopped finally. All this was in 1945, after the atomic bombs.

In January 1946, my 18th birthday was on the 18th. My mother said, "The war is over (both wars). Let's celebrate your 18th birthday." We invited my girlfriends and other people (can't remember). We cooked a lot of goodies, but nobody showed up. They all had something else to do on that day, but there were no telephones, so we never were informed. We had to throw a lot of good food away.

I finished high school in 1947. My favorite subjects were algebra and geometry. I was already married, and my name was Mrs. van der Upwich when I graduated from high school."

THE OCCUPATION

CHAPTER 5

The Japanese Imperial Army occupied the
Dutch East Indies from March 1942 until
the end of the war in September 1945. The
period was one of the most critical in the
history of the Dutch East Indies and would
change it forever.

The Dutch East Indies had been a colony of
the Netherlands (the Dutch) since 1800.
However, the Netherlands in Europe had
been occupied by Hitler's German Army in
1940, and thus had little ability to defend
its colony against the Japanese Imperial
Army. Less than three months after the
first attacks on Borneo, the Japanese navy
and army overran Dutch and allied forces.
Initially, most Indonesians welcomed the
Japanese as liberators from their Dutch
colonial masters. This sentiment quickly
changed however, as approximately 5
million Indonesian citizens were taken
away from Indonesia as forced laborers for
Japanese military projects, including the
Burma-Siam railway where my Dad spent
3 ½ years. Four million people died in

Indonesia as a result of famine and forced labor during the Japanese occupation, including 30,000 European civilian deaths. Japan's World War II occupation dismantled much of the Dutch colonial state and economy. Following the Japanese surrender in August 1945, Indonesian nationalists declared independence which they fought to secure during the subsequent Indonesian National Revolution. The Netherlands formally recognized sovereignty of the United States of Indonesia at the 1949 Dutch–Indonesian Round Table Conference with the exception of Western New Guinea, where my parents and many others fled to and where I was born. This territory was transferred to Indonesian authority via the United Nations 13 years later in 1962. My family left in 1960 and immigrated to the United States of America.

When they invaded, the Japanese Army rounded up all white Europeans on the island and sent them to camps to keep them under control and prevent an organized revolt. The women and children were segregated from the men in different camps. The men were systematically shipped out to Southeast Asia to work on the railway supply lines or build other infrastructure for the Japanese military. My mother and her friends the De Jong brothers were of Dutch and Indonesian heritage, but looked indigenous enough to be left alone and spared them the fate of starvation in the camps that many faced for a period of almost 4 years. The indigenous citizens were allowed to move around with strict limitations. Many were recruited by the Japanese Army to work, or for intelligence and security.

In the camps, thousands either died or were malnourished to as low as 50% of their original body weight by the time they were liberated in 1945. I met and knew Frits De Jong during the 1990's after my father passed away. He was a kind and generous man to a fault and he still loved my mother 50 years later. I traveled back to Indonesia with Frits and my mother. He was a man who everyone loved. He and my mother dated for many years until his death in the early 2000's. I got to tour the land that was the birthplace of my parents and it was fascinatingly unlike any place I could have imagined. I regret never personally thanking Frits for what he did to protect my mother during these dangerous times.

My mother always said that she married my father because he was ruggedly handsome and he was a very capable, confident man who she felt safe with and protected. He was a man's man. Knowing her, I saw why that was important after a life of much uncertainty, fear and danger.

HERMAN CORNELIS LOUIS

CHAPTER 6

A woman is anxiously whipping the horse pulling her buggy for many miles down dirt roads in the middle of the night. She and her two children are attempting to escape the falling debris and hot mudflows coming from the eruption and violent explosion of the volcano Mt. Kelud, 100 miles to the east. In the end an estimated 5000 people perished in East Java, Indonesia.

Its 1919, and Kelud has erupted again hurling boulders, hot ashes, and spewing rapid mudflows as far as 200 miles to the west. Mudflows, known as "Lahars," mix with water and debris. They move very rapidly destroying everything in their path much like flooding waters. The eruption is only one of many recorded throughout history in East Java dating back hundreds of years. Eight year old Herman Van der Upwich and his sister are safe thanks to his mother who had bravely driven that buggy from disaster and fled the path of destruction. The family was visiting friends in East Java and the delay to return to Bandung almost cost them their lives. Little Herman grew up to be a handsome man, educated and a confident leader. As a young man, he was quite the lady's man and he worked in management for the plantation companies of Central and East Java growing coffee, tea and tobacco. These commodities were exported to the Netherlands and the rest Europe.

The green rolling hills on the island of Java stretched for miles with coffee and tea plantations along the roads and would disappear over the hills as far as you can see. Everywhere you look tobacco leaves are drying in the sun on rooftops. There are no tractors or modern farm equipment. These endless stretches of perfectly tilled rows were planted by hand and plowed by Oxen still in 1995 when I was there. My father passed away in 1991, but I couldn't help but feel his presence as I gazed out onto similar plantations he worked, and the land he loved.

Herman enlisted in the Royal Dutch Army KNIL Reserves as a militia soldier on June 6, 1933 in Bandung, Java. This was traditional for young men in those days. The Dutch Army paid for enlistment as a reservist much like we do in America with our own Army National Guard of which my brother served for 6 years.

KNIL Militia Soldiers

"Louk" (pronounced Luke) as Herman was known, remained a reservist for 8 years serving 3 week training commitments every two years. He was born in Bandung, and his mother still resided there. With the Japanese military on the move in the Pacific, he was called into active duty December 1, 1941 and assigned to the 2ND Landstorm Battalion in Surabaya.

It's December 10, 1941. Japan is on the move southward after attacking Pearl Harbor, Hawaii on December 7th, and regrouping to move into South East Asia. The allied forces made up of Australian, Indonesian, British and Dutch forces hurriedly organized to repel any attempt by the Japanese Army to invade the East Indies.

BATTLE OF EAST JAVA

CHAPTER 7

The darkness of night lightens and dawn appears to the east as the sun starts to peek above the watery horizon of the Java Sea. It's March 1, 1942 and Allied Forces await the arrival of the Japanese forces.

The Java Sea is an extensive shallow sea on the Sunda Shelf. It lies between the Indonesian islands of Borneo to the north, Java to the south, Sumatra to the west, and Sulawesi to the east. Karimata Strait to its northwest links it to the South China Sea. It is a part of the western Pacific Ocean.

The Allied forces were commanded by the Royal Netherlands East Indies Army General Hein ter Poorten.

Although the KNIL forces had on paper 25,000 well-armed troops, many were Indonesian and poorly trained. The KNIL forces were deployed in four sub-commands: Batavia area (two regiments); north central Java (one regiment); south Java (one regiment) and east Java (one regiment). Corporal Herman Van der Upwich was in the east Java regiment out of Surabaya, the 2ND Infantry Division, Landstorm Battalion.

The Japanese troops landed at three points on Java on March 1ST. The Japanese West Java invasion convoy landed on Bantam Bay near Merak and Eretan Wetan. The West Java convoy had previously fought in the Battle of Sunda Strait, a few hours prior to the landings.

Meanwhile, the Japanese East Java invasion convoy landed on Kragan after having defeated the ABDA (American-British-Dutch-Australian) fleet in the Battle of the Java Sea. Hundreds of Allied lives were lost.

By March 7th, defeat was inevitable with the town of Tjilatjap already in Japanese hands. Surabaya was being evacuated while Japanese troops were rapidly converging on Bandung.

At 09:00 on March 8TH, the Commander-in-Chief of the Allied forces, General Hein Ter Poorten, announced the surrender of the Royal Netherlands East Indies Army in Java. Herman was taken captive in Bangkalan, East Java on March 8, 1942.

At 23:00, the Dutch radio station NIROM (Nederlandsch Indische Radio Omroep Maatschappij) broadcast the last news from a temporary transmitter at Ciumbuluit. The announcer Bert Garthoff ended the broadcast with the words "Wij sluiten nu. Vaarwel tot betere tijden. Leve de Koningin!" (We are closing now. Farewell till better times. Long live the Queen!) As history records, those better times will be short lived and the Dutch East Indies will be changed forever.

This plaque honoring Herman's military service is displayed at Mt. Soledad Veterans Memorial in La Jolla, California

PRISONER OF WAR

CHAPTER 8

In March of 1942, the Japanese landed on the island of Java and overran the allied forces. Herman and thousands of others in military service to the Netherlands were captured and sent to labor camps. Tens of thousands were sent to Burma to work on a land route called the Burma Railway that would connect Bangkok with Rangoon in Burma to move supplies to the Japanese military in the East Indies. Herman was one of them. After a grueling rail and boat trip, they walked for days to reach several outposts along the river. Those who were already wounded when taken prisoner died under the strain of the heat, lack of food, water and rest.

The mosquitoes and humidity was relentless. Every time Herman slapped one off his sweaty, sun burned face, three more were biting his sunburned neck. Back and forth it went after dark until daybreak. Peaceful sleep was impossible. The sweat and dirt of 6 days marching through jungle and mountainous terrain had taken their toll in more ways than one. Johann, another Corporal in the Royal Dutch Army was breathing hard and gasping for water, severely dehydrated after vomiting all day and lacking nutrition beyond a cup of rice. At daybreak, a Japanese soldier would come by with an old wooden water bucket. The men would clamber and reach for it like it was a rope on the edge of a cliff. Water was dispersed only twice a day and with temperatures and humidity in the 90's, the jungle could choke a water buffalo. Men, who could no longer go on, were left to die in the stifling heat. There is nothing sadder or more heartbreaking than hearing a dying man plead for help and weep like a baby for mercy in the distant as you march off under threat of being shot. The cries become faint and you hope the suffering stops by way of quiet death in this merciless place. It's something you never forget. You feel a combination of anger and utter despair, but then the instinct to survive takes over. This was Burma, a God forsaken jungle of overgrowth and thorny undergrowth that ran alongside Malaysia to the east and the Indian Ocean to the west. The Japanese wanted to build a railway supply line through this rugged terrain for their forces in the East Indies.

The camps were far from livable. Prisoners cut and fashioned bamboo for racks to lie down or sit. Commodes were holes in the ground. Heavily guarded around the clock, some men tried to escape. The Japanese made a sport of who could shoot the escapee first before fellow prisoners buried him.

Powerful bonds formed among the prisoners. Meager rations were shared with desperately ill comrades and prisoners sometimes risked their lives to barter outside the camps to help others. There were Red Cross doctors who were ill equipped to deal with the malnutrition and diseases. They had to improvise medical equipment while drugs were denied to them by the Japanese. War prisoners in the Far East were seven times more likely to die than those captured in Europe.

Although escape was attempted out of desperation, it was almost impossible. Most camps were hundreds of miles from Allied-held territory. Prisoners were under nourished and unable to survive for long and Europeans outside the camps in Asia would easily be noticed.

Did I mention that the Japanese were already coming to Indonesia in the 1930's? In Bandung, Luke's sister was a school teacher. Over the years, she had many Japanese students in her classes. These students were the children of diplomats, dignitaries or well to do from Japan, and many socialized with the teacher's family and were part of the community, much like an exchange student. They were there to learn about European education and culture.

When jobs were assigned in the camps, Luke was assigned to drive a truck between labor camps to shuttle food staples, water and building materials. Initially feeling just lucky he was assigned a job that could possibly aid in his survival, Herman didn't realize for months the camp Lieutenant was a young Japanese officer who had recognized him as the brother of his past teacher in Java. That quiet action helped save his life and allowed Herman to steal a little food for himself and his comrades. If caught, a severe beating awaited the perpetrator. Snakes and rats were regularly caught, cooked and eaten for protein. The rice, water and meager supply of vegetables were not enough to survive. Men started to appear skeletal, and thousands died from dysentery and malaria coupled with malnutrition.

The task of burying the dead was a daily task and a necessity to prevent the further spread of diseases. By the time the railway was completed, 160,000 malnourished military and civilian prisoners were still in the labor camps. The construction project lasted from June 1942 to October 1943. 102,000 military and civilian laborers died. Conditions were horrific. Herman had developed Beriberi, but survived. Beriberi is a disease caused by a vitamin B-1 deficiency, also known as thiamine deficiency. Beriberi damages the nerves and can lead to decreased muscle strength and eventually, muscle paralysis and is usually brought on by malnutrition.

After the completion of the railway (16 months), many prisoners were assigned to work parties destined for Japan or periodically returned to Burma for railway maintenance or repairs. A large number of prisoners remained in Thailand base camps until the end of the war working to cut wood for fuel or other projects for the Japanese.

When President Harry Truman dropped the bombs on Hiroshima and Nagasaki in August 1945, he saved the lives of 160,000 POW's and liberated millions of civilians. Sadly, sometimes only catastrophic force can stop evil. The Japanese Army surrendered and laid their arms down in the camps. My father told me that before the bombs were dropped, prisoners were ordered to dig long trenches in the camps. Communications intercepted by the CIA went something like this:

"We don't need these prisoners anymore. What do we do with the workers?"

Reply from Japan's Emperor: "Shoot them". The long trenches were to be mass graves.

I asked him, "what happened after the Japanese guards laid down their arms and surrendered to the prisoners?" My father didn't answer and changed the subject. That was his style. He was very reserved.

An American engineer who viewed the railway project after the war said, "What makes this an engineering feat is the totality of it, the accumulation of factors. The total length of miles (258), the total number of bridges (600), including six to eight long-span bridges, the total number of people who were involved (250,000), the very short time in which they managed to accomplish it, and the extreme conditions they accomplished it under. They had very little transportation to get stuff to and from

the workers, they had almost no medication, they couldn't get food let alone materials, they had no tools to work with except for basic things like spades and hammers, and they worked in extremely difficult conditions in the jungle with its heat and humidity. All of that makes this railway an extraordinary accomplishment."
One of the bridge projects was the subject of a Hollywood movie, "Bridge on the River Kwai."
Three cemeteries maintained by the Commonwealth War Graves Commission (CWGC) contain the vast majority of Allied military personnel who died on the Burma Railway. These memorials can be visited today to honor the following lives that were lost.

6,609 British	3,143 Dutch
2,697 Australians	33 members
of the Indian Army	
5 New Zealanders	2 Danes
9 Canadians	

THE MEETING

CHAPTER 9

My parents, Herman and Marie were newlyweds living in his birthplace, Bandung, on the island of Java. He met her while driving a city bus in Jakarta. The war was over and he was liberated. He spent some time in Thailand recuperating from August 1945 till March 1946, but he was still serving in the military for a paycheck and to assist in reconstruction. He was assigned to driving city buses as well as military vehicles as the country was attempting to gain some normalcy and rebuild. Wherever the need in a chaotic time, the military was there. My Mom was a bus passenger on her way to work at her new job, also contributing to repair the destruction. When the newly formed United Nations arrived, humanitarian aid and medical assistance was brought in. In the previous 4 years of military occupation, families were dispersed throughout numerous camps on Java and divided according to gender and race. My Mom got a job going through hundreds of 3x5" index cards and other records to help families locate lost members and help reunite them. My Dad noticed this young attractive, very shy passenger and spoke with her. It turned out they knew some of the same people. At a community dance a couple of months later, a girlfriend of hers introduced her to the handsome military man who drove the bus as "Louk" (pronounced Luke). It was love at first sight for both and they were inseparable. As I stated, my dad was still serving in the military to aid in the stabilization of the country and was stationed at an Army base near Batavia (Jakarta). As the story goes, he had to smuggle her on base where he lived hidden under blankets and bags on a military truck so they could be together. My dad was still legally married, but in divorce proceedings. Many came back from the war to discover their spouses had made life changes. When he was liberated and returned home, he found his former wife was involved with another man. Knowing he was sent to the labor camps in Burma, she figured he was dead and moved on.

My Mom and Dad got married in a simple garden setting. In the only wedding day photo in existence on the next page, he was still wearing his military fatigues. When he was discharged from the Dutch Army, they were living in Bandung, his birthplace. When I traveled to Indonesia in 1995 with my mother, she showed me the house and garage where they ran a taxi business and auto repair shop from 1946 - 1947. Jakarta is 120 miles from Bandung and many people traveled back and forth needing transportation.

MANOKWARI TO AMERICA

CHAPTER 10

The western half of New Guinea, known today as Western New Guinea was retained by the Dutch government after World War II. My parents, Herman and Marie Van der Upwich were among many who fled the island of Java and migrated to New Guinea attempting to keep the familiarity of the only life and country they knew. The migration of new settlers was big as homes, small farms and rustic towns sprang up out of the jungle along the northern coast. A peaceful, prosperous and free way of life continued for these Dutch / Indonesian families until 1959.

President Sukarno, a dictator who ruled with force in Indonesia after the changeover, aligned himself with communists like Khrushchev of the Soviet Union. There isn't much difference between communism and tyranny. It takes one to achieve the other. Just look at Cuba or Venezuela.

"Luke" (Herman's nickname) came home one day to tell Marie he had bad news. The Netherlands, still weak from the war in Europe, capitulated to avoid violence against the Dutch/Indo settlers who inhabited the northern coast of New Guinea. Indonesian President Sukarno, with assistance from the Soviet Navy wanted western New Guinea as well. The Soviet Navy was already patrolling off the coast awaiting orders.

Luke and Marie worked hard all those years, establishing a chicken farm, building a general store that sold imported goods, and even Honda scooters. They had to leave the life they loved and the people they loved "again". In a scouting trip/vacation my parents made in 1959, they stopped in Texas to visit a friend from the East Indies who was married to an American. In a twist of fate, the gentleman offered to sponsor our family to immigrate to the United States. He found out Luke was a foreign car mechanic and the gentleman loved foreign cars long before they were popular in America. That was the only way you could come to America in those days.

The departure day arrived too soon, with Marie in tears and heartbroken. Luke was stoic. The airfield outside of town was basically a tin building serving as a terminal once used by Allied Forces during the war. With the Ford Tri-Motor warming up, friends and family gathered to bid a tearful farewell. They flew off into those warm trade winds bound for Sydney, Australia, hoping for a secure future with their 4 children (one unborn). I still remember looking out the window of the plane and marveling at the site of lights below in the darkness of night as we approached mainland Australia.

There, we boarded a passenger ship to America. That ship was later renamed the Achille Lauro. Yes, the famous one in the news in 1985 when it was hijacked by terrorists. In the next 24 months, almost everyone of European descent left the East Indies for good.

The journey that sent this family halfway around the world through the Panama Canal, the language and cultural barriers, the disappointments and challenges are something I can attest to with certainty, because Luke and Marie are my parents.

Their incredible lives rubbed off on me, and the reality that you can accomplish much in life if you apply yourself is something I saw with my own eyes growing up. Were there tough times and adversity? Absolutely. Luke and Marie became successful real estate investors and business owners. There were no entitlements. There was good luck and there were people who made a difference. It's always about people. Even after losing everything in the first two years in America after a bad investment, their hard work and perseverance got them through and much more. Dreams do come true.

IDA MATHILDA CHOMPFF

CHAPTER 11

"There is a God and I thank him for re-
uniting my family and keeping us from
perishing."
These are the words of my Grandmother,
Ida Chompff.
The following story and events are shared
from her writings. She endured personal
tragedies, extreme poverty and survived a
horrific war and invasion of the land she
loved. Chaos that turned her life and the
lives of millions upside down resulted in
the deaths of millions of innocent people,
but her faith carried her through.
Ida was born June 1910. Her mother,
Christina Wilhelmina Gordon was half
English and half Javanese and born in
1878. Ida's mother, Christina was a
beautiful girl. Ida's father, Rudolf was a
Baron from Switzerland and a member of
Swiss nobility.
Ida's father traveled from Switzerland to
the Dutch East Indies for business and
Boar hunting regularly. This was around

1905-1910. According to her mother, one of those Boar hunting trips almost resulted in tragedy. He was an avid Boar hunter. Ida's mother would have to skin the animals and salt the meat to preserve it. There were no freezers or refrigerators in those days. On one of those trips while tracking a Boar by himself, he was attacked by a Bengal tiger that sprung from a tree overhead. When he did not come home, Ida's mother organized a search party to look for him. It was not unusual for people to disappear in the jungle and not be seen again in those days. Luckily he was found alive hours later. His back was ripped open and the Tiger was lying dead next to him with a knife plunged into its chest. In 1911, Ida's father Rudolf died of an unrelated and unknown illness.

Its 1925 and the world had just stopped reeling from the conflict in Europe known as WWI. Ida was living in what many would consider paradise. If you have ever ventured beyond the city lights and traffic jams of Western Civilization to places like the Caribbean Islands or Tahiti, you would get a feel for the Dutch East Indies. Balmy weather, lots of humidity and insects so large and plentiful, you could take them for pets and name them.

Of course there are the beautiful gentle swaying palm trees and the warm tropical winds in your face. It's a very unspoiled, exotic place on Earth.

My grandmother Ida was the youngest of seven children. She had two older sisters and four older brothers. Her mother remarried in 1917 to a man who worked at a plantation. He was a good man and treated Ida's mother and the children very decently. Her mother never forgot Ida's father, Rudolf or stopped loving him.

Ida with her mother Christina and her first two kids (Dee & Marie my mom)

The island of Java was colonized by Europeans. For generations there was the white educated class with the native Indonesians employed as blue collar labor, house keepers and nannies. Many were extended family of their employers and even lived on the same property. There was no class strife as one might imagine due to the fact the native Indonesians standard of living was greatly raised with gainful employment, until a couple of decades later. Many had never experienced a ride in an automobile, or saw modern communication and radios.

Like many societies throughout history where you have the co-mingling of two different cultures, you are going to get intermingling. The Indonesian women were beautiful. The European men found them irresistible and of course marriage of the two different races produced children. This went on for generations. I am the product of such a phenomenon with my European father and my mother who was part Javanese and European.

My grandmother Ida and her family lived in a house too far from school, so she moved in with her older sister Marie, whom my mother was named after. I never knew this until I started working on this story. Ida's sister Marie was married and lived closer to school. It was still pretty far, but she traveled there by train daily. Marie and her husband lived on the south coast of Java in a small town named Kalisat. She lived with them for about 2 years to attend school. There was no school near the plantation where her mother Christina and second husband lived. Every morning, a Bendi (carriage drawn by single horse), took her to the train station so she could take the train to school miles away. From there she walked to school and back in the afternoon. The same Bendi brought her home from the station as well. The wait could exceed an hour or more since the train was often late. Thankfully there was always a woman selling Nasie Rawon for 10 cents. Nasie Rawon is a bowl of rice with black soup, meat and spices.

That same year 1925, my grandmother Ida was on vacation at the home of her sister Leida who lived in Tjilatjap a nearby town. Ida's mother came unexpectedly. She had just returned from a trip to East Java. Without any explanation she announced

"I come to take you back with me to Bondowoso". Bondowoso is a town in East Java, where she now lived. Ida's sister Leida asked, "Why so sudden, Ma?" Ida's mother looking a little embarrassed said, "There is a man who would like to meet your sister Ida, and I promised him I would bring her back with me". Leida was angry but realized there was nothing she could do to stop it. Ida's mother visited a few more days and then Ida and her left for Bondowoso where Ida's step father and his 2 younger sisters lived. When Ida arrived in Bondowoso, she was greeted by her older sister Marie. She too was angry to find out about this pre-arranged meeting with this man. Ida's mother made the decision and that was it.

Ida asked her mother how this man knew of her. Apparently he had seen a picture somewhere although Ida had no idea where or how this would happen. The man's name was Chris Chompff. He was 20 years older, a widower and had 5 children between the ages of 6 and 12. An older woman went with Ida to be introduced.

Ida later in life was troubled by this event in her life. She regretted letting others make life decisions for her. At the time she was exactly 15 ½ years old.

The day came for Ida to pack her clothes and her 'husband to be' took her to the home of his younger brother Adrian who worked on a sugar plantation in Probolingo. In those days it was improper to have the girl you want to marry live under the same roof with you till after your wedding day. Chris had to wait for time off from work for the wedding, so that's why Ida had to stay with Adrian and his wife.

When Chris came to pick Ida up from his brother's home, he acted strange and a little cool towards his brother. Someone had spread rumors that Adrian and Ida were having an affair which was unfounded and baseless. Ida was being chaperoned and cared for by another older woman during this time. Chris was a jealous man. Ida and Chris were married in Bandung.

In 1926, Ida gave birth to her first child, Theodora (Dee). Her second was born in 1928, Marie Antoinette (my mother). Her third child died at 3 months old. It was now 1930 and the world was in an economic depression when Ida's fourth child was born, Alfred (Fred). Ida and Chris had to relocate to Malang where they downsized to a two bedroom small house with no furniture and everyone had to sleep on the floor. Boxes were used as tables to eat. They lived with 4 children from Chris and two new babies. Ida still found joy in her life and family regardless.

Ida's older sister Marie moved to Batavia
during these hard times. When Fred was
10 months old, Ida and her children moved
in with her mother in Wlingi. There was no
money. Ida and Chris had used all his
savings from the company he worked for.
Ida and her children stayed with her
mother for about 6 months. One day Chris
visited and said his brother had a vacant
house the family could live in. This area
was known as the Kampong. It was very
poor, far from town and the buildings
were very old and in disrepair. Ida and her
family did move there reunited with Chris.
Chris refused to accept his brother's free
help. Instead he used his life insurance
savings. Ida had a wonderful year. The
children were happy playing around the
houses and bathing daily in the river.
Chris and his brother Eugene went pig
hunting on weekends. It was Ida's job to
skin the animal and preserve the meat by
salting it. There was no refrigeration, but it
was good to eat meat again.
Eugene found Chris a job in Pekalongan as
a bookkeeper. Ida and her family moved to
Pekalongan. This house was bigger, was
not furnished but did have beds. Everyone

was relieved to be back in a bed again rather than sleep on the floor.

In 1935, Ida was pregnant with a son Rudy. This birth was a breach and the labor went on for hours and hours. Chris urged the midwife to call a doctor in, but she resisted and basically said, "I got this". After the baby was born, everyone was relieved. Chris showed Ida a revolver he was carrying. She asked him why he was carrying a gun? He said that if anything happened to her or the baby, he was going to shoot the midwife who resisted calling a doctor. When Rudy was 2 years old, Chris passed away. He had a bad heart and caught influenza.

When his co-worker visited him lying in bed sick, Chris said "don't worry, I'll be back at the office". Those were his last words.

After the funeral, Chris' brother Adrian let Ida and kids live with him for a while, but later had to move back to Batavia and back to the Kampong district, an area that resembled a ghetto or slum. The family lived there for about a year. It was a difficult time until Ida's sister offered to let the family live with her near Batavia. There was no money, no jobs, no husband. These were trying, difficult times.

One day Ida was walking down the street and she noticed a tailor shop. She asked the shop keeper if there was any work available. The shop keeper asked Ida if she knew anything about tailoring European clothes. She said, "a little". Ida was tested and it came out very well. She started her new job making 25 guilders a month. In those days it was plenty for a family. They could eat on 10 guilders a month and rent for a suitable house in a decent area was 10 guilders. To earn extra money, Ida repaired or made clothes for friends as well. It seemed that finally the family got a break.

FROM PLANTATION

TO PRISONERS

CHAPTER 12

December 7, 1941. The attack on Pearl
Harbor, Hawaii changed everything.
America declared war on Japan and all hell
broke loose the following months.
In weeks, the Japanese Army took the
Philippines, went south to Burma,
Singapore and Malaysia. From there they
jumped to Sumatra, Dutch East Indies. As
the days passed, Japanese planes were seen
flying over Java. It was all so strange and
very unreal. The only Japanese Ida ever
knew were always very polite and
friendly. But from now on Japan was the
enemy. One day, a Japanese plane came
over and machine gunned two men
working on the roof of a building in town.
Children had to be rushed away
immediately and everyone was running
for cover before he could turn back and do
it again. There was fear and panic.
On Sunday, February 15, 1942, Ida and her
family received the bad news over the

radio that Singapore had fallen. Then there was the Battle of the Java Sea from February 27th to March 1st. The Dutch warships Ruyter and Java were hit by Japanese torpedoes; they sunk with a huge loss of life. The Allies lost this naval battle. On March 8, 1942, the Dutch Army on Java surrendered to the Japanese Imperial Army.

On March 9th, Ida and family were looking through the windows into the streets. The Japanese entered the city. They came on bicycles or were just walking and carrying rifles. They looked terrible, all with some cloth attached at the back of their caps and they looked very strange.

This was a kind of Japanese Ida had never imagined. The Japanese pushed their way through Java. All Dutch men were put in jail or prisoner of war camps. Dutch women were put in women's camps.

The local nuns went to the chapel daily to pray for all those living in the Dutch East Indies, but it appeared the Dutch East Indies was lost forever.

Ida and kids were spared the fate of the camps, but she stayed out of sight. She immediately went to work baking cookies and other baked goods to survive. The boys took care of the order taking from people in town and collected the money. They also went to the markets to purchase ingredients to keep the baked goods coming so the family could eat.

In the camps people became sick and there was no medicine. There was not enough food and Ida and her neighbors were under constant control of the Japanese Guards in the area. After almost 4 years of occupation, the Japanese Army surrendered after Nagasaki and Hiroshima were leveled when the atomic bombs were dropped by order of U.S. President Harry Truman.

Months later, Chris' brother, Adrian came and found Ida. Ida did not recognize him at first. Crying, she hugged him after realizing it was truly him. Ida had already accepted the fact he was probably dead. Adrian was in the Netherlands when the war broke out in Europe. He was taken prisoner of war in Germany. After the war and liberation, he volunteered to join the British troops heading back to Indonesia. He came back to the woman he secretly loved and never forgot. He told his wife he would start divorce proceedings when back in Indonesia. He looked around the small crude house Ida and her kids were living in and said, "We are going to find another house".

Ida had no idea where Dee her first child was after the war ended. She told Adrian she was worried about Dee. He said he would try to locate her. Word came that Dee was sick and living in the Kampong area. There were native Indonesians who were sympathetic to the Dutch who had been brutalized by the Japanese Army. Ida always felt these acts by the locals was a blessing from God. The reunion was overwhelming. Dee told stories of a lack of food and money, and sickness of the children. Dee sadly told a story about how hungry the kids were and she could not stand it anymore. She had to make the decision to slaughter her pet goat. She cried when sharing the story and so did Ida. Dee moved in with Ida and Adrian and so did Ida's daughter Marie (my mother), and Ida's sons Fred and Rudy. My mom's boyfriend Frits De Jong who took care of her during the war years also came, but left soon after for a Seaman's job on transport ships moving rice from Thailand to war torn Java.

Adrian got an offer to work on the island of Bangka, so Ida and he left for Bangka with sons Rudy, Ronny, and Albert. Ida's ninth child, Louis was born April 1947. Ida and Adrian were married on August 13, 1947. Adrian legally adopted Ronny and Albert who were from a previous relationship. When Louis was 9 ½ months old, Ida and Adrian moved back to Batavia (soon to be Jakarta). A couple of months later they moved to Bandung, where Ida's newly married daughter (Marie) and my dad Herman Van der Upwich lived. Ida was now expecting her 10th child. My mom and dad, Herman and Marie were making plans to go to New Guinea to build a new life. They were planning to bring some livestock like chickens and a couple little pigs. Indonesia was on the brink of being independent and the native population did not like the Dutch. This rapidly coming period was known as the "changeover". Many in the native population were incited to believe that the Europeans were evil and used them.

Adrian got a job offer from the government on the island of Morotai. Ida was 6 months pregnant with her 10th child. Adrian went first and when he found a house, Ida followed with the kids.

"I found the man I truly love. This love that brought me waves of good feelings makes my heartbeat faster just from thinking about him, my man, my life, my love. Can a woman ever love a man so much as I love him?" These words were expressed in writing by Ida about Adrian.

Ida & Adrian

The future for Ida and the children looked much brighter. After they settled, the baby was born. It was a girl. They named her Irene.

After some time the family moved back to Jakarta and plans were made to travel to New Guinea where my mother and father settled and were building a new life. Before Ida and Adrian left for New Guinea, Adrian was offered a job to demolish and remove war machinery and debris on an island close to New Guinea. The problem was there was no school for the boys. However, my mother and father offered to take them into their home in New Guinea while Adrian completed this project.

Ida and Adrian were now living on the island of Pediwang where he was working. One day, a man approached Ida and had a little boy with him. The boy had a large open wound on his leg. The man said, "excuse me ma'dam, can you help us? My son cries every night and we cannot stand to hear him suffer anymore." Ida looked at the wound and was shocked. "What do I have in my medical supplies?" she thought. She found a bottle of Permagaan, a disinfectant solution. She let the boy sit on a chair with his leg stretched out on another chair. She started washing off the wound with the solution and let the solution go through the wound. Shockingly, she could see the bone in his leg. She kept washing the wound till it looked fresh. From old linen she wrapped the wound and told the man to bring the boy back the next day. The next day they came back and the father said the boy had a good night. Ida gave the boy the same treatment every day for the next week and could see some improvement in the condition of the wound. The wound got smaller and smaller and soon was healing. A couple of days later the man came with a plate of rice and some money he wanted Ida to have. Ida only accepted his offering out of respect for his desire to thank her. Word got around, and one day a woman came over. She told Ida she suffered from diarrhea. Ida looked in her medical supply bag and gave her a treatment. After some time, people started coming. Ida's house looked like a medical clinic. Ida asked Adrian if she could get a ride to the island of Tobelo so she could get more supplies.

Adrian looked very surprised. "Do you know what you are doing?' he asked. "Why not send them to Tobelo?" Ida reminded him that these people do not have any money for a doctor. Adrian did not like this, but agreed. The wound of the little boy eventually completely healed. The front veranda of Ida's house looked like a clinic with many patients. Soon after Ida and Adrian left the island and went back to Jakarta for a short time to plan their trip to New Guinea.

They arrived in Manokwari where I was born. My dad built a small house for Ida and family in Wosie, a small village where my mother and father kept a chicken farm. The house was one room built from Bamboo and one wall was heavy canvas material left over from the war. It was meant to be temporary. After they arrived, my dad helped them build another house. My mother started a small grocery store in the front room of their own house in Manokwari. Soon even the Papua natives came to spend their hard earned money at the store. Business was good as the only grocery and durable goods mercantile in the area. When Ida and Adrian finally arrived in New Guinea, they were shocked at the hard work that was ahead for them since the town of Manokwari was very small and undeveloped.

One day Ida craved bread. There was no bakery on the island so she decided to find a way to bake her own bread. A 5 gallon metal can was located. She cleaned it, and bored holes around it for ventilation. Ida then started looking for yeast or flour. Above all odds, ingredients were located somewhere. She started with burning wood to make hot coals. Then the metal can was put on top of the hot coals. The dough was put into a small bake pan that was in her travel stuff. That day, she ate the best tasting bread in the whole world. Ida shared her desire to start baking bread to sell, so Adrian built her a real wood fire oven made from bricks. Soon everyone knew they were producing bread and in came the orders. Adrian was offered a job for the government on the island of Biak, an island in the bay just offshore. Ida and Adrian moved to Biak. There the bakery lived on and grew into a commercial operation. As a child, I spent a summer on Biak with Oma Ida and Opa Adrian. I

remember the bakery. I was 5 years old.
The name of the bakery was "Bakery Bush
Bush" and soon was hiring local people to
keep up with demand that included a
Dutch Marine Battalion on the island as
clients.
Years passed. My mother and father
worked hard and saved for many years. In
1959, they went on an extended vacation to
the Netherlands, America and other
destinations. This trip doubled as a
scouting mission for the next move our
family would make. Ida and Adrian were
preparing to move to Holland
(Netherlands). As mentioned in other
places in this book, political pressure and
threats from authoritarianism required the
relocation of my family one last time. The
bakery was sold when Ida and Adrian
went to Holland. Ida and Adrian were
living in Holland and took in her mother
Christina who was suffering from
Alzheimers and Dimentia. Christina, my
great grandmother passed away in 1963 at
the age of 84.
In 1964, Ida and Adrian came to California
to visit us and saw what a wonderful place
America is. In 1965, they immigrated

permanently, sponsored by their son, Ronny Chompff who was in the United States Army. Unfortunately, Adrian passed away soon after. Ida lived till 2001 and enjoyed decades with her large reunited family in the United States. I was at her funeral and will never forget the size of the crowd who came to honor this incredible lady. Always the happy face in the room, she was a loving and caring person her entire life, and she made the best authentic Dutch baked goods and deserts that were an unforgettable part of my childhood.

Ida & 7 of her children 1968

HERMAN'S AUTO SERVICE

CHAPTER 13

My parents received a settlement for my dad's military back pay from the Dutch Government in 1965 for his years in Burma as a POW. I believe the amount was close to $5000. That was a lot of money in the 1960's.

When this settlement was received, my father was working for Jims Union 76 located at the corner of Springdale St and Bolsa Ave in Huntington Beach, California. He serviced cars in the garage and also pumped gas to assist the guys working the driveway when things got busy. He was like that. He was a team player. In those days, everybody received full service from a driveway attendant that included pumping the gas and washing the front and back windshield. If a customer wanted, checking tire pressure in all 4 tires and fluids under the hood was performed. It was important to check the water in radiators during hot weather. Automotive engineering was basic. I don't remember seeing coolant used in radiators till much later. Instead of buying new tires for your car, you could purchase cheaper retread tires. That is where a new rubber tread was pressed on worn out tires by a heat compress process. The problem is on hot asphalt highways, the rubber retread could come loose. These tires were banned a few years later.

My parents had an opportunity to purchase the lease of a Gulf service station in Fountain Valley, California located at the corner of Warner Ave and Magnolia St. This was the big break in their lives to achieve independence and take control of their own destiny. I started working there after school when I was 15. My mother would pick me up from home in the afternoon and I would help out for 3-4 hours daily. This was a promotion for me from the paper route I had since I was 11 years old. I was now earning $1 an hour in a world where the lawful minimum wage was $1.25. This was 1969 and gasoline was about 30 cents a gallon. In a VW, a dollar of gas got you around for days. People would pull into the gas station and ask for a "bucks worth of regular". One day, I walked out to help a guy in a Cadillac and it was Alan Hale Jr., the skipper from Gilligan's Island. I pumped $5 worth of gas for him. He said he was on his way to a party in Newport Beach.

Some of my friends in high school worked at the gas station. It was cool. At night when business was slower, we could work on our cars in the garage and use the hydraulic lift. Try that today. Naught!

My friend Harold who worked at the gas station through high school and college told me John McCain came in for gas with his sister after he was released as a North Vietnamese captive. His sister lived in the area. We all had long hair like our favorite 70's rock & roll bands in those days and apparently the future Senator and Presidential candidate had some comments for Harold regarding his shoulder length hair and how his appearance was unacceptable.

In those days, there was not only bias towards people that looked different, but there was considerable bias towards hippies and rock & roll. The times they are a changin' as Bob Dylan used to say.

The gas station was some of the best years of my life and I didn't even know it.

After I left for the mountains of Northern California in 1975, things happened with the gas station. Gulf Oil Company decided they would exit the retail gasoline business in California and were not going to renew leases. My folks had worked hard and done pretty well. Two options were available to lessees. The property would be sold by Gulf and the business would close. Option # 2 was you had to buy the gas station and land from Gulf Oil. My parents went after option #2. My mother successfully obtained an SBA loan, but had to put up their home as collateral as well. The purchase price was $250,000. They took the risk, and the gas station was renamed to "Herman's Auto Service". Business went along as usual. My older brother got involved in a more committed role to the business and gave up his pursuit of being a full time police officer. This was about 1978. Property appreciation boomed in Southern California for the next ten years. My parents had a friend Dan who was a realtor. He provided guidance on how to buy homes in the area for rental property, so my parents did. My mother was instrumental in this very astute decision. My parents were savers. They did not buy expensive things for themselves. My dad never owned a new car. My mother never owned a luxury car in her life. Expensive furniture or the latest electronics and expensive jewelry were just not important. Personal gratification in the way of materialism was not in their DNA. They bought "used" and were happy.

The land and neighborhood around Herman's Auto Service started to become developed. The city of Fountain Valley and Huntington Beach were booming with housing, business developments and prosperity.

They say the outcome of someone's life can come down to two or three decisions. As the years went by into the 1980's, the corner of Magnolia and Warner in Fountain Valley became the focus of much business, shopping and traffic. People who knew my dad used to come by and ask him, "Hey Herman, when are you going to sell this property and retire?" My dad who was not easily impressed or swayed always replied with a sarcastic remark, "when they pay me a million for it". Well, about 1987 someone did offer to buy that property for $750,000, and my folks agreed to take their offer. Little did we know we would lose my dad in 4 short years later. He was starting to feel the down side of chronic emphysema that he was diagnosed with in 1960 from smoking. I can remember going places with him and he had to stop to catch his breath so he wouldn't pass out. I'm sure he knew his health was taking a turn for the worst and he wanted to make sure my Mom was financially set for the years she would be without him. When he died, she was only 63 years old. When he was on oxygen and housebound, I visited him one day and we were watching television. He got my undivided attention during a commercial break and made me promise to not allow him to deteriorate in a nursing home. He told me to "accidently" kick the respirator machines electrical cord out of the wall. I agreed just to appease him, because I had no idea what I would do. He did not want to die in a way that caused unneeded anguish or long term suffering for my mother, his sweetheart of 45 years. He always looked out for her first. The strong man, the rugged warrior and survivor in him was something I always had great respect for and as his son I could not understand what he went through in his life during the war years. In fact it frightened me just to think about it as a child. In 1991, my mother called me and said, "this is it". My dad had been bed ridden for a few days in the house. He stopped eating and was just laying peacefully. My sister, an RN and I were with him when he passed that same day. I got my final wish to show him that I loved him by holding the hand of one of the most courageous, selfless men I had ever known as he passed. You know, he never bought himself that red 1959 Chevrolet Impala convertible with white interior and it just seemed wrong on some level.

When my mother passed in August 2016, I still had his ashes in an urn. I had carried it around between 6 different residences over 25 years. We put his remains in moms casket and the circle was completed so that they both were together again. My mother always regretted cremating him, so when she got sick I made a promise to her to put his remains in her casket. Herman and Marie Van der Upwich are buried together at the Westminster Memorial Park in Westminster, California. A lot of my extended family is there. Ida Mathilda Chompff, my grandmother is there as well. So is her son and my mother's brother, Fred.

UNCLE RON

CHAPTER 14

Ronald Chompff was born in 1940 on Java,
Dutch East Indies. He was my uncle and I
loved him because he was so unpredictable
and goofy. When we lived in Huntington
Beach in the early 1960's he would
hitchhike (thumb a ride) from Ft. Hood,
Texas where he was attached to the U.S.
Army 2nd Armored Division "Hell on
Wheels". He would come to visit my
mother and us kids. I once questioned him
about the sensibility of hitchhiking all that
way. I remember him saying that no one
dared attempt anything stupid since he
always hitchhiked in his Army uniform.
And if he were to go missing, the U.S.
military would spare nothing to find him.
Really?
One time he came to visit and he had a
very visible scar on one side of his
forehead. He was accidently shot during a
live fire exercise at Ft Hood. He was
crawling under barb wire with bullets
zinging overhead. A bullet caught him in
the head. He almost died in surgery but

pulled through. He later told me he experienced the "other side" where people go when they die. I didn't know whether to believe him. I was maybe 12 years old. I need to emphasize that he loved my mother, the woman who looked out for him and was there for him always. My mother was the world's greatest big sister to him. Ron used to live with us in New Guinea. He was only 10 years older than my own brother, so he was like one of the kids. He was fun and threw caution to the wind. This was a trait I subconsciously adopted in my life and I'm glad I did. He was someone you were happy to see. He laughed a lot.

He used his U.S. Army privilege to sponsor his parents Ida and Adrian's immigration to America. One of my earliest recollections of him was when he took us kids to see "Help", the Beatles movie at the drive-in theater. We saw the movie twice and didn't get home till 2 am. The drive-in would run it twice a night in those days. This was 1965.

When he got out of the Army, he attended night school to earn a degree in mechanical drafting. There were no computers in those days. One time when he applied for a job, he was asked if he knew about designing hydraulic systems and he said yes, so they hired him. Actually he didn't know hydraulics, so he spent a few days at the library reading and studying hydraulics. When he reported for the job, he was able to struggle through the work and if stuck, he would ask an associate for assistance claiming he misplaced his reference material. He told me this story with a smirk on his face and I learned that sometimes "going for it" in life works out. Years went by. Uncle Ron married and had children. He used to stop by my Moms house in Huntington Beach on his BMW motorcycle when I was in high school. He was driving a motorcycle daily through 75 miles of freeway gridlock each way (150 miles total) from his house in Lake Elsinore, California to El Segundo near Los Angeles for his job at Lockheed Aircraft Co. He did this for years! Humorously, I thought maybe the bullet to the head did more damage than people realized. This is who he was. He did what he wanted. Ron had a love for flying so he earned a private pilot's license to fly small planes like Cessna's. This happened while I was living in Northern California. He told me that on a trip back from Central California, he encountered heavy fog. In order to fly legally in those conditions you have to be instrument rated as a pilot and he wasn't. He decided to just fly low over the 5 freeway towards Los Angeles and follow the car headlights he could see below. When he got to his destination at Burbank Airport, people were yelling to him to stop the plane. The rear rudder and tail section of the plane were almost ripped loose. He was later contacted by the FAA. He somehow had struck high power lines north of Los Angeles and taken out power to about 5000 homes. He added that he remembered feeling a jolt in the aircraft while flying back. Long story short, his license to fly was revoked for life. Did I say he loved to fly? For the remainder of his life, Ron owned a sophisticated computer flight simulation set up in his home. He loved aircraft and he loved to fly.

I visited him in Tarpon Springs, Florida in 2003. He had just retired from Lockheed in Atlanta, Georgia. He spent years in Atlanta and was a highly respected aircraft systems designer. He moved to Florida for a fresh start after some setbacks.

He seemed lost, but we had a good time. Ron once told me that the culmination of his life can be illustrated like this: When he was a boy in Java after WWII, he would stand in a field bare footed and look up in the sky with wonder as military jets flew by. That same bare footed boy grew up to be selected to review and sign off on the final blueprints for the Lockheed Martin F22 Raptor fighter plane. This plane is capable of flying 1500 MPH.

Ron and Joanie

Ronald Chompff passed away September 2017. I believe the death of my mother a year prior affected him in a very adverse way and contributed to his failing health. I miss him and will always regret not getting the chance to see him one more time before he was gone so I could tell him how he influenced my life.

IMMIGRANT VIBES

CHAPTER 15

This wonderful place called America is a
land created and built by immigrants from
all over the world. Nearly all Americans
are descendants of immigrants seeking a
better life starting with America's
founders.

They come to our shores, enhance our
labor force, become entrepreneurs who
hire more people providing jobs and
opportunities for others. They reinvigorate
our work force and they bring diversity
and culture.

There have been times brought on by fear
of change, and fear of contrary traditions
that resulted in policies not consistent with
these American values. For the most part,
immigrants want the ability to worship
freely, free speech without government
retribution, and the freedom to direct their
own economic success just as the
forefathers of this great country desired
and established as a promise in our
founding documents.

Much of our economic success can be attributed to immigration. Over half of American startups with a value over 1 billion dollars are founded by immigrants. Job creation, the promotion of innovation contributes mightily to America's economic success. They come to embrace the same values and disciplines that resulted in a success story for native born Americans.

They may not forget where they came from and that is ok. It's because of their past lives that motivate them to embrace our values and opportunities. My parents and many of our extended family enjoyed their traditional foods and continued to speak Dutch as their first language even though they spoke English as well. That diversity along with other cultures who feel free to continue what they know from their past is what makes America strong.

Immigrants know all about a lack of opportunity to make money. It's why they come to America. Free enterprise allows immigrants who come here to start a business for themselves as small as a food or beverage cart. Many wind up starting blue collar businesses like landscaping, automotive services, restaurants, construction, etc.

Policies of over-regulation and high taxation of incomes, sales tax, and regulatory fees inhibit opportunity for the lowest income entrepreneurs and stifles growth. Free enterprise is a gift and immigrants know this. That's why many open their own businesses. My parents did and they were staunch supporters of politicians who were against socialist policies of high taxation.

This is what I call a "GIBI". Good Intention, Bad Idea. Yes, I coined that acronym. A lot of politicians are full of GIBI's and one other thing that stinks. Socialism is GIBI.

It's about equality they say. Yeah, the equality of shared misery. When you raise income taxes on corporate America, big companies simply raise prices to compensate for it. The result is consumers pay more. The wealthier consumer can easily pay more. The low income worker / small business owner gets hurt with higher prices and taxes they cannot easily absorb. It's another fallacy of GIBI. The intent of helping the less fortunate actually winds up hurting the less fortunate. See how that works? See how that doesn't work?

Here's a prime example of GIBI. The California legislature tried to destroy the ability to make money driving in the 'shared ride' industry as an independent contractor. The fallacy was that independent contractors were being used by greedy corporations who provided no benefits. There was almost zero support from the actual drivers for this legislation. This would have affected hundreds of thousands of self-employed people. The company that owns the software and infrastructure to allow this free enterprise was going to pull out of California if the legislation was upheld. Thankfully the voters righted this wrong and stopped this intrusion into personal freedom. This is another example of misguided do-gooders guilty of a major GIBI.

Despite what you may hear from right wing politicians, America needs workers. Immigrants contribute to American businesses and the economy in many ways. They work hard and can make up more than a third of the workforce in many industries. Their mobile ability helps businesses fill worker shortages as in agriculture and manufacturing. Immigrants support the aging native-born population in home care, elderly facilities and maintenance industries. Workers also contribute to and bolster the Social Security and Medicare trust funds we all benefit from. Children of immigrant families are upwardly mobile and contribute future benefits to not only their families, but to the nation's economy as well.

I once read an article in the Orange County Register challenging people who have a problem with non-citizen workers and laborers to imagine their lives without affordable lawn care services, car washes, in home care services, construction, painting, tree trimming, etc. I have been in the residential remodeling business for many years. I can attest to the fact that this industry would suffer greatly without the workers who do everything from hauling debris, roofing, concrete work, demolition, stucco and all phases of construction. It is hard work and I have personally done it. There would be a major labor shortage affecting costs and the timely completion of projects. The notion that these job labor shortages could easily be filled by American workers born here is a fantasy.

INTERESTING PEOPLE

CHAPTER 16

My neighbor in Alderpoint, California was
an artist named Frank. Alderpoint
residents were primarily local Indians who
worked at the lumber mill and rednecks.
There was only a small store, post office
and no gas station. Garberville was 18
miles over a mountain range so you had to
make sure when you went home to
Alderpoint, you had enough gas to make it
back. In those days I had an interest in
pencil sketching people's faces while
painting signs in Garberville.
My neighbor Frank Cieciorka was an
accomplished water color artist and a cool
guy. He used to come over and give me
pointers about what I was doing and it was
much appreciated. He lived in a small
wood framed house he built himself in
1972. It was very rustic with basic comforts
like wood heat. Years later I looked him up
on the internet. It turns out Frank was an
important civil rights activist in the 1960's.

In 1957, Frank joined the Socialist Party while attending San Jose State College out of opposition to American military intervention in the Dominican Republic and later Vietnam. In 1964, he volunteered as an organizer during the Freedom Summer drive to register black voters in Mississippi and served as field secretary for the Student Nonviolent Coordinating Committee. Frank also helped organize the Mississippi Freedom Democratic Party, an alternative to the official white-dominated state Democratic Party. Segregation was an accepted practice.

Examples of political art go back to about 1917. One day Frank saw a raised fist used as a symbol at a Socialist rally in San Francisco. He decided it was prefect for a woodcut.

Woodcut is a relief printing technique in printmaking. An artist carves an image into the surface of a block of wood — typically with gouges — leaving the printing parts level with the surface while removing the non-printing parts. The surface is covered in ink with a roller. Then the image can then be pressed onto a poster or flyer. The clenched fist gained widespread popularity when Frank and friends made buttons and thousands were passed out at political rallies and demonstrations. The symbol was picked up immediately by Students for a Democratic Society. The Black Panthers used it in their publications as a "power salute".

Frank and his first wife Bobbi, wrote and illustrated a book titled "Negroes in American History; A Freedom Primer". The book was used in freedom schools throughout the south in the early days of the civil rights movement. Frank also used the clenched fist in poster art for the United Farm Workers in the 1960's. He was also art director for The Movement newspaper. Frank settled in Alderpoint, California in 1972 and became a noted water color artist. I saw his work and was amazed at how beautifully detailed it was. Frank died from emphysema in November 2008 in Alderpoint in that little wood framed house he built. He was a wonderful neighbor, a kind and giving man. Most importantly, he lived a free life and he worked for a noble cause so others could as well.

****

Larry Ethridge was born the same year as Elvis Presley, 1935. I met Larry in 1974. He had a building filled with second hand Americana collectables and western items passed on from Knotts Berry Farm in Buena Park which was undergoing a major makeover. These items were otherwise destined for the dump. This building was in the old part of Huntington Beach next to the railroad tracks near Gothard St. Larry also built and painted signs and partnered with Don Treece on many hand painting sign projects. Don Treece was graphic arts director at Knott's Berry Farm at a time when Knott's was only a replica western ghost town with restaurants, farm animals, simple amusement rides and attractions. Larry gave me the opportunity to start hand painting signs and learn the trade. I was thrilled. I could smell the freedom of self-employment as an "artist". This type of work was very appealing to me. It was colorful, bold and outdoors.

I apprenticed with Larry for 3 years with no pay and was happy to do so. I lived with him and his family and went with the Ethridge family to the mountains of Northern California in 1975. I had an opportunity to find my own way in life, free of outside pressures and expectations. I had a ball. I will always be grateful to Larry and his family for the camaraderie, love and opportunity to live an adventure I would not otherwise have lived. I was only 20 years old at the time.

Larry called me one day in 1992 and asked me if I would like to join him in a project for a comedian and part time Tonight Show host named Jay Leno. Of course I jumped at the opportunity. Larry's school friend from his youth became Jay's full time mechanic / machinist at his shop in Burbank, California. "Mike", was a retired motorcycle sidecar racer and spent years restoring vintage motorcycles as a hobby. Jay also collected and restored motorcycles, so he hired Mike to run day to day operations in Jay's early days of car and motorcycle collecting.

In those days, we were sworn to secrecy as to Jays shop location. It was disruptive to have strangers lurking around and worse trespassing.

Larry was my best friend and a mentor. He was a very talented man in many ways and courageous. He is the only person I ever knew who represented himself in a superior court jury trial and won against a state prosecutor. Larry was not an attorney. I told Larry I would always love him in a phone call in 2008. It was obvious we had gone our separate ways in attitudes and goals. Larry passed away in 2013 at the age of 78.

****

I met Fred Bradfield in Garberville,
California. He was working as a bartender
at the Branding Iron Saloon next door to
the hardware store I worked at. This was
1981 and Garberville was enjoying an
economic boom due to the millions of
dollars flowing into the area from the
Cannabis business. By now Southern
Humboldt County was famous for its
"product". The hardware store and lumber
yard where I was assistant manager was
making record annual sales in growing
supplies. It was a ritual to stop by the
Branding Iron after work for a beer.
Fred and I became fast friends. I found out
Fred was a sound engineer for the Grateful
Dead. The Branding Iron was one of 3 bars
in a town with two gas stations and 2
grocery stores. A year later Fred
approached me and asked me if I was
interested in playing "roadie" for a band
called New Riders of the Purple Sage. This
was a band Jerry Garcia co-founded and
was an associate act. The bands lead singer
and songwriter was John Dawson
"Marmaduke". He and Jerry go way back

in the San Francisco music scene. In those years, the two bands hosted a traditional New Year's Eve concert in San Francisco. My job was to drive to San Rafael, California and pick up a van with $500 cash under the floor mat in the middle of the night. I had to meet the band at Calgary International Airport in Canada on a given date and time. I had about 3 days to get there.

This was a trip of 1300 miles. I took some time off work and off I went to the land where everyone says "Eh?" The Canadian Rockies were a spectacular sight and very desolate with small towns in the middle of nowhere.

The van was needed on the bands tour for equipment purposes. I met them at the airport and the bands manager arranged a hotel room, etc. for me. I got to know John Dawson on this trip. The life of a band on the road is different. Waking hours are from about noon till 2-3 am. The band was made up of John, Pat Shanahan and Billy Wolf who were from Rick Nelson's Stone Canyon Band, Buddy Cage who came from Ann Murray's band, Allen Kemp, and David Nelson who recorded with the

Grateful Dead as well. Surprisingly, they were not the crazy rock and roll type. All were working family guys with mortgages. When I had to fly back home, John invited me to visit him and his wife in Larkspur, California. It just never happened, but it was a fun experience while it lasted. I met up with John again in 1982 when the band came to So. Humboldt County for a concert. John Dawson passed away July 2009 from lung cancer in Mexico where he retired.